Know Your Buses

James Race

Old Pond Publishing

First published 2010

Copyright © James Race, 2010

The moral rights of the author in this book have been asserted

ISBN 978-1-906853-38-9

Published by:
Old Pond Publishing Ltd
Dencora Business Centre
36 White House Road
Ipswich IP1 5LT
United Kingdom

www.oldpond.com

Book designed by Liz Whatling
Printed and bound in China

Contents

*A*cknowledgements

I would like to thank Syd Eade, Jonathan Whitlam and everyone else
who has helped in producing this book.

*P*icture Credits

Syd Eade: 1, 9, 10, 16, 19, 20, 24, 26, 27, 28, 33, 34, 35, 37, 38, and 43
All other photographs are from author's own collection

*A*uthor's Note

Names and models of chassis and body types are included for identification purposes only.
All information is given in good faith and should be used as a guide.
The author cannot be held responsible for any errors.

Foreword

In all corners of Great Britain buses can be found transporting the public every day, both for local and longer distance runs, as well as sightseeing and school transport.

In this book I show the operators' most popular choices in vehicle acquisitions as well as a few more unusual models. This being said, all the vehicles featured are currently licensed for public use.

As the information on the left hand side of each vehicle's page shows, many chassis are built in countries different from their bodywork. Surprisingly, this also applies to integral buses which are not always complete when departing the country of origin.

'Traditional' buses had the engine located at the front of the vehicle over the front axle often with an open platform at the rear. During the 1960s and early 1970s it became increasingly common to find vehicles with their engine located at the rear of the chassis. This enabled the entrance door to be placed at the front making it possible for the driver to collect fares. These days none of the traditional type has survived in everyday passenger service, the survivors being restricted to 'heritage' and other special services.

JAMES RACE
Lowestoft 2010

AEC Routemaster

Chassis
Assembled/Manufactured in:
United Kingdom

Bodywork
Assembled/Manufactured in:
United Kingdom

The AEC Routemaster is probably the best known red London bus. These vehicles were designed jointly by London Transport and AEC to meet London's requirements, and very successfully as some of the buses were still serving the capital when nearly fifty years old.

Most Routemasters were delivered with AEC's own 9.6 or 11.3 litre engines, although many were subsequently replaced during their long service life with newer designs from other manufacturers. Power steering was standard from new as was a Wilson automatic gearbox. This was sometimes retained when vehicles were re-engined.

Routemasters are integral vehicles with aluminium frames. They were originally available in 26 ft 6 in and 30 ft lengths, the latter having a characteristic half-size centre window. Many variations of Routemaster exist. Standard service buses were joined by express coaches, front-entrance versions towing trailers and a solitary rear-engine model.

Blue Bird AARE

Chassis
Assembled/Manufactured in:
United States of America

Bodywork
Assembled/Manufactured in:
United States of America

Blue Bird is the manufacturer of the American school buses imported for the First Student UK operation. The AARE, which stands for All American Rear Engine, looks typical of the yellow school buses seen in films the world over.

The AARE has a Cummins ISC-07 engine coupled to an Allison 6-speed automatic gearbox. Optional extras include a large fuel tank, mud flaps, vandal locks and air suspension.

Blue Bird's own 60-seat bodywork is shown with American-style simulated traffic lights painted on the front and rear. In America traffic may not pass the bus in either direction when the lights flash, a great road safety feature. In the UK it is not legal even to have the lights fitted.

BMC 1100LE

Chassis
Assembled/Manufactured in:
Turkey

Bodywork
Assembled/Manufactured in:
Turkey

The BMC 1100LE, also known as the Falcon, is probably BMC's best known production service bus.

The 1100LE has a Cummins ISBe engine coupled to a Voith automatic gearbox. It has a 'C'-section steel profile chassis frame and is fitted with 'kneeling' suspension as standard.

The vehicle shown has BMC's own 40-seat stainless steel bodywork resulting in a gross vehicle weight of 17,000 kg.

4

Bristol VR

Chassis
Assembled/Manufactured in:
United Kingdom

Bodywork
Assembled/Manufactured in:
United Kingdom

Very few production vehicles have been so different from its prototype as the Bristol VR. The original design was the VRL which had the engine longitudinally mounted in-line with the chassis behind the rear axle. The VRT, however, has it transversely mounted across the rear of the chassis and accounted for almost all the production.

The VRT had either a Gardner or Leyland engine connected to a semi-automatic or fully automatic gearbox.

As shown, the usual bodywork for the VR was built by Eastern Coach Works. Other choices included Northern Counties, Alexander, Willowbrook, East Lancs and MCW.

DAF DB250

Chassis
Assembled/Manufactured in:
Netherlands

Bodywork
Assembled/Manufactured in:
United Kingdom

Description

The DB250 was launched by DAF and later joined the VDL product range. The design has since been incorporated into the Wright Gemini 2.

The DB250 is powered by one of DAF's own engines coupled to either a Voith or ZF gearbox. The DB250 is the step-entrance chassis. Low-floor models were later available and known as DB250LF.

Optare were the original company to body the DB250 with their Spectra bodywork as shown on the bus in the photograph. Other manufacturers included Northern Counties, Plaxton, Alexander and East Lancashire.

DAF SB220

Chassis
Assembled/Manufactured in:
Netherlands

Bodywork
Assembled/Manufactured in:
Hungary

The SB220 was designed to be a city bus and has now been replaced by the DAF and VDL SB200 and SB250. The SB220 comes in both step-entrance and low-floor models.

The SB220 has a DAF 8.6 litre engine usually coupled to a ZF automatic gearbox, although a Voith unit was available. SB220s are between 11 and 12 m long and 2.5 m wide.

The vehicle shown has an Ikarus Citibus step-entrance body. Other options available are Optare Delta and Northern Counties Paladine. Low-floor bodies include Alexander ALX300, East Lancs Myllennium and Ikarus Polaris.

Dennis Dart

Chassis
Assembled/Manufactured in:
United Kingdom

Bodywork
Assembled/Manufactured in:
United Kingdom

Description

The Dennis Dart is a small, conventional rear-engined chassis designed to have a stepped front entrance.

The Cummins B series engine with an Allison automatic gearbox was standard. The design was originally 2.3 m wide and 9 m long although London Buses received an 8.5 m model so that it could be treated as a minibus for licensing regulations. Very soon the Dart also appeared in lengths from 8.5 m to 9.8 m.

The Dart was launched with the Duple Dartline body design, which was sold to Carlyle and later passed to Marshall of Cambridge. However, most Darts received the Plaxton Pointer body. Other options available were Alexander Dash, Wright Handybus, East Lancs EL2000, Northern Counties Paladin and Wadham Stringer Portsdown.

Dennis Dart SLF

Chassis
Assembled/Manufactured in:
United Kingdom

Bodywork
Assembled/Manufactured in:
United Kingdom

The Dennis Dart SLF is the low-floor cousin of the standard step-entrance Dart. The chassis was also later sold under the names Transbus Dart and Alexander Dennis Dart.

The SLF was originally offered with the same running gear as the step-entrance chassis with a length of 9.2 m, 8.8 m, 10 m, 10.6 m and shortly afterwards 11.3 m. To make the bus 'Euro III' compliant all lengths have as standard a Cummins 3.9 litre engine, except the later 11.3 m which had a 5.9 litre unit, driving either an Allison or Voith gearbox.

The bodywork shown is a Marshall 'Capital' which was also later built in small numbers by MCV. Other bodies for this chassis include Plaxton's low-floor Pointer and Pointer 2, East Lancs Spryte, Wright Crusader and Alexander ALX200.

9

Dennis Dominator

Chassis
Assembled/Manufactured in:
United Kingdom

Bodywork
Assembled/Manufactured in:
United Kingdom

The Dominator was the first venture Dennis made into the rear-engined bus market and was also the first double-deck bus chassis to be produced since the Loline in the 1960s.

Dominators are powered by a choice of Cummins L10, Rolls-Royce Eagle or Gardner 6LX unit driving a Voith or ZF automatic gearbox.

Alexander, East Lancashire, Marshall and Northern Counties all built bodywork for the Dennis Dominator chassis. The picture shows an East Lancs product.

Dennis Dragon

Chassis
Assembled/Manufactured in:
United Kingdom

Bodywork
Assembled/Manufactured in:
Kenya

Description

The Dennis Dragon was a tri-axle version of the Dennis Dominator. The Dragons were designed for Kowloon Motor Bus (Kowloon roughly translates to 'nine dragons'). However, when an order was received from the rival China Motor Bus the name 'Condor' was used to prevent 'naming for an opponent company'.

Dragons and Condors had a Gardner engine, with Cummins as an option, later becoming standard, coupled to either a Voith or ZF automatic gearbox.

The vehicle shown has a Duple Metsec body, as do most Dennis Dragons. This vehicle was new to Stagecoach Kenya in 1996 and was returned to the United Kingdom in 1998 for Stagecoach Manchester's Magic Bus fleet.

Dennis Enviro200

Chassis
Assembled/Manufactured in:
United Kingdom

Bodywork
Assembled/Manufactured in:
United Kingdom

Description

The Alexander Dennis Enviro200 Dart, to give it its full title, is designed to be a successor to the Dennis Dart SLF and Plaxton Pointer body.

The chassis is available in lengths between 8.9 m and 11.3 m with a Cummins four- or six-cylinder engine and a choice of either an Allison or Voith gearbox. A hybrid drive option is available utilising the BAE system which promises thirty per cent reductions in fuel costs and exhaust emissions.

The Enviro200 Dart is an integrated concept produced by Alexander Dennis. However, the Enviro200 body is also available on a MAN 14.240 chassis.

Dennis Enviro400

Chassis
Assembled/Manufactured in:
United Kingdom

Bodywork
Assembled/Manufactured in:
United Kingdom

Description

The Alexander Dennis Enviro400 was designed by Transbus International as a replacement for the Trident and the Alexander ALX400 body.

Enviro400s have a Cummins six-cylinder engine with either Voith or ZF transmission. A hybrid option is available equipped with the BAE system.

The Enviro400 is also available as a model of bodywork in its own right and can be found on Volvo B7TL, B9TL and Scania chassis.

Dennis Enviro500

Chassis
Assembled/Manufactured in:
United Kingdom

Bodywork
Assembled/Manufactured in:
United Kingdom

Like the Enviro400, the Alexander Dennis Enviro500 was designed by Transbus International. It is currently the largest of the Enviro-series bus designs produced by Alexander Dennis.

The Enviro500 has a Cummins engine coupled to either a Voith or ZF gearbox, with an Allison unit later becoming available as an option. A hybrid version is also available utilising GM-Allison's 'Parallel Hybrid' drive which claims to cut fuel costs and exhaust emissions by over twenty-five per cent.

The vehicle depicted has the standard Enviro500 body with a capacity of nearly a hundred seated passengers. As usual for Enviro products the body can also be fitted to other chassis – in this case the Volvo B9TL's tri-axle version.

Dennis Lance

Chassis
Assembled/Manufactured in:
United Kingdom

Bodywork
Assembled/Manufactured in:
Netherlands

Description

The Lance is a full-size city bus designed as the replacement for the Dennis Falcon.

The Lance can be found in either step-entrance or low-floor variants. It has a Cummins engine driving a ZF gearbox. The Lance was later also made available as a double-deck chassis called the Dennis Arrow. The Arrow did not, however, enjoy the same success as the Lance.

Bodywork for the step-entrance models of the Dennis Lance include Alexander PS and Plaxton Verde. Low-floor models have many styles of bodywork including the Wrights and Berkhof, the latter carried on the bus shown in the photograph.

Dennis Trident

Chassis
Assembled/Manufactured in:
United Kingdom

Bodywork
Assembled/Manufactured in:
United Kingdom

The Dennis Trident is a low-floor chassis which replaced the Dennis Arrow. The Trident design later passed to Transbus before finally being dropped from production by Alexander Dennis.

The Trident chassis is powered by either a Cummins Euro II or Euro III engine driving a Voith or ZF gearbox. Tridents are available in lengths between 9.9 m and 11.4 m, and are 2.55 m wide.

Plaxton's President is the bodywork shown; other options available include East Lancs Lolyne and Alexander ALX400.

Irisbus Agora Line

Chassis
Assembled/Manufactured in:
France

Bodywork
Assembled/Manufactured in:
France/United Kingdom

The Agora was designed by Renault. The design later passed to Irisbus, a joint venture between Renault and IVECO, with the latter company now having sole ownership.

The Agora Line is 12 m long and powered by a longitudinally mounted IVECO engine coupled to either a Voith or ZF gearbox.

The bodywork shown is the standard Irisbus-completed vehicle. Optare also offer a body on this chassis and, although very few have been built, the two manufacturers' products are indistinguishable.

17

Leyland Lion

Chassis
Assembled/Manufactured in:
Denmark

Bodywork
Assembled/Manufactured in:
United Kingdom

Description

The Leyland Lion dating from the 1980s is an underfloor-engined chassis built by DAB for Leyland. It was always unusual to find them in service as only just over thirty were sold. However, despite this, Lions are still to be found in use on school and contract services.

The Leyland-DAB Lion was powered by either a Leyland 680 or TL11 engine with gearbox options including ZF, Self-Changing Gears or Wilson transmissions. The Lion's overall length is 10 m with a wheelbase of just over 5 m.

The bus shown was built by East Lancashire Coachbuilders, while other Lions were bodied by Alexander and Northern Counties.

Leyland Lynx

Chassis
Assembled/Manufactured in:
United Kingdom

Bodywork
Assembled/Manufactured in:
United Kingdom

Leyland designed the Lynx to replace the National. Like its predecessor, the Lynx has had a service life lasting much longer than originally anticipated.

The Leyland Lynx could be fitted with either Leyland, Gardner or Cummins engines coupled to either a Leyland or a ZF gearbox.

Very few Lynx buses received bodywork different from the example shown which was built by Leyland themselves. The Lynx II is easily recognisable as it has a bulbous front grille as opposed to the more flush appearance of the original front area.

Leyland National

Chassis
Assembled/Manufactured in:
United Kingdom

Bodywork
Assembled/Manufactured in:
United Kingdom

Description

The Leyland National was designed by British Leyland for the National Bus Company to replace the large and varied selection of single-deck designs inherited from its constituent companies.

Leyland's National was available in two lengths: 10.3 m and 11.3 m. A feature of most Nationals is the characteristic pod mounted above the rear windows which houses a heating and ventilation system. The original National was fitted with Leyland's own highly turbocharged 510 engine, although the later National 2 had the option of either a Leyland 680 or Gardner 6HLXB coupled to a ZF or G2 gearbox.

The Leyland National is an integral vehicle of modular construction designed for easy replacement. Some operators which refurbished their Nationals fitted them with DAF or Volvo engines.

Leyland Olympian

Chassis
Assembled/Manufactured in:
United Kingdom

Bodywork
Assembled/Manufactured in:
United Kingdom

Description

Leyland's Olympian was designed as a conventional body-on-chassis vehicle for operators not wishing to buy into the integral design of the modern style bus.

Engine options for the Olympian include Leyland's own TL11, Gardner's 6LXB and Cummins' L10 with gearbox options from Leyland, Voith and ZF.

An almost identical looking body style was produced by Leyland, Eastern Coachworks, Roe and Optare at various times. Other bodybuilders were East Lancs, Marshall and Alexander. The bus in the picture is a Northern Counties product.

Leyland Titan

Chassis
Assembled/Manufactured in:
United Kingdom

Bodywork
Assembled/Manufactured in:
United Kingdom

Description

The Titan was designed and built by British Leyland. Production started at the Park Royal works in London, later moving to Leyland's Workington plant.

The Titan has either one of Leyland's own engines or a Gardner 6LXB driving a Leyland gearbox. They were only produced in one format, 9.5 m long by 2.5 m wide.

The bodywork was Leyland's own design, its most distinctive feature being the large half-width rear window. The one shown has been converted to open-top form and is seen here in use on York City tours after its service life finished in London.

MAN 14.220

Chassis
Assembled/Manufactured in:
Germany

Bodywork
Assembled/Manufactured in:
United Kingdom

Description

The MAN 14.220 chassis was designed for city bus work and has since been superseded by the MAN 12.240.

The 14.220 has one of MAN's own engines driving either a ZF or Voith automatic gearbox. The model number is an indication of the engine's horsepower rating, which in this case is 220 hp.

The Evolution bodywork is produced by MCV Bus and Coach, a subsidiary of the Manufacturing Commercial Vehicles Group based in Egypt. Other bodywork options include Alexander, East Lancashire Coachbuilders, Marcopolo and Plaxton.

23

MCW Metrobus

Chassis
Assembled/Manufactured in:
United Kingdom

Bodywork
Assembled/Manufactured in:
United Kingdom

The Metrobus is an integral vehicle designed and built by Metro-Cammell Weymann in substantial numbers.

The Metrobus was offered with either a Gardner, Cummins or Rolls-Royce engine driving a Voith or Maxwell gearbox.

The MCW-built Metrobus is easily identifiable by its nearside windscreen being larger than its offside. However, despite being an integral product, Metrobuses can also be found with Alexander and Northern Counties bodies.

Mercedes O405

Chassis
Assembled/Manufactured in:
Germany

Bodywork
Assembled/Manufactured in:
United Kingdom

Description

The O405 has been built in both low-floor and step-entrance configurations and was eventually replaced by the Citaro in the Mercedes product range.

O405s have a Mercedes engine fitted as standard, attached to a Mercedes, ZF or Voith gearbox. The O405 also comes as an articulated model – the O405G.

The vehicle shown has an Optare Prisma body. Wrights produced a very similar looking body for the O405, made possible as the entire front end is supplied by Mercedes.

25

Mercedes O814D

Chassis
Assembled/Manufactured in:
Germany

Bodywork
Assembled/Manufactured in:
United Kingdom

Description

The Mercedes-Benz O814D is a member of the Mercedes Vario family. The O814D variant is a van-derived chassis modified for minibus use.

The O814D has a 4.25 litre Mercedes diesel engine coupled to either a ZF or Allison gearbox. Both manual and automatics were produced. These step-entrance vehicles are 2.3 m wide and 8.5 m long.

The vehicle shown has a Plaxton Beaver 2 body which is available with either bus or coach seating. A mobility option is also available with a wheelchair lift located towards the rear.

Mercedes Citaro

Chassis
Assembled/Manufactured in:
Germany, France, Spain

Bodywork
Assembled/Manufactured in:
Germany, France, Spain

The Mercedes-Benz Citaro is designed to be the replacement for the O405 and O405N series of buses. This low-floor vehicle comes in a bewildering number of variations and is also popular in mainland Europe.

Whether your Citaro is a rigid or articulated vehicle, it will have one of Mercedes' own engines driving through either a Voith or ZF automatic gearbox. For those operators wishing for a manual gearbox Mercedes-Benz can provide one of their own units. The Citaro can also be powered by natural gas engines and hydrogen fuel cells. A hybrid electric drive is also available.

Two different designs of bodywork styling are available. One has an angled destination display while the second has a one-piece windscreen which covers the destination equipment.

27

Optare Excel

Chassis
Assembled/Manufactured in:
United Kingdom

Bodywork
Assembled/Manufactured in:
United Kingdom

The Excel is a low-floor integral vehicle that was eventually replaced by the Optare Tempo.

Excels come in two varieties: the Excel and the Excel 2 built in lengths between 9.6 m and 11.8 m. These have either a Cummins or a Mercedes-Benz engine and both options have an Allison automatic gearbox.

The bodywork is made of all-welded steel box section, with modular front and rear fibreglass panels. The side panels are fitted with an 'Easy Lock' system to make accident repairs quick and simple.

Optare Solo

Chassis
Assembled/Manufactured in:
United Kingdom

Bodywork
Assembled/Manufactured in:
United Kingdom

The name Solo comes from Optare's claim that with kneeling suspension the entrance is 'so low' with a 200 mm ground clearance. Two distinct variations can be found in the United Kingdom. The vehicle shown is a standard Solo. The Solo SR however has similar body styling to the Optare Versa, although its specification is unchanged.

The most noticeable characteristic is the forward position of the front wheels, with the entrance behind them. The Solo is offered as standard with a 4.25 litre Mercedes engine, although options are a 5.90 litre Cummins or 4.58 litre MAN engine. All have a 5-speed Allison gearbox. An electric option is also available with an Envoa Zero Emissions drive.

Between the two variations there are eight different lengths ranging from 7.1 m to 10.18 m. Both SR and standard models are available in slimline form, meaning the overall width is noticeably reduced.

Optare Tempo

Chassis
Assembled/Manufactured in:
United Kingdom

Bodywork
Assembled/Manufactured in:
United Kingdom

Description

The Tempo is a lightweight integral, designed to replace the Excel in Optare's product range.

Tempos are available in four standard lengths: 10.565 m, 11.275 m, 11.985 m and 12.605 m. Most are powered by a Mercedes-Benz 6.73 litre engine. Options are a MAN 6.871 litre unit or an Allison Hybrid Drive System. Conventional gearboxes are an Allison 5-speed or a ZF 6-speed, both with lock-up torque converters.

The bodywork is a combination of fibreglass- reinforced polymer and aluminium panels on a stainless and carbon steel welded box-section frame. Maximum seating capacity ranges from 35 to 47 depending on the length of the vehicle.

Optare Versa

Chassis
Assembled/Manufactured in:
United Kingdom

Bodywork
Assembled/Manufactured in:
United Kingdom

Description

The Versa is easily identified by the large windscreen design that sweeps into the roof-mounted pod when viewed from the sides. The 'pod' feature is to house an air-conditioning unit irrespective of whether or not it is specified.

The Versa's standard engine is a Mercedes 4.25 litre unit, with a Cummins 5.9 litre or MAN 4.58 litre unit available as options, driving through an Allison 5-speed automatic gearbox.

The front and rear bodywork sections are glass-reinforced plastic, with metal side panels locking on to rail sections with screw fasteners. The Versa seats between 36 and 40 passengers and is intended for use as a front-line low-floor bus.

Plaxton Primo

Chassis
Assembled/Manufactured in:
Hungary

Bodywork
Assembled/Manufactured in:
United Kingdom

The Primo was designed to be a low-floor accessible Minibus with a wheel base of 4.4 metres and its total length under 8 metres. It is manoeuvrable without compromising on passenger space.

Primo buses are integral vehicles. The underframe is supplied as the Plasma by Enterprise Bus, utilising a Cummings ISBe 140B 4-cylinder engine connected to an Allison 2000 series 5-speed automatic gearbox and a special Z drive to the back axle made by Raba.

The stainless steel frames are finished by Plaxton using fibreglass for the front and rear with aluminium detachable side panels. Maximum passenger capacity is 28 seats.

32

Scania N113CRB

Chassis
Assembled/Manufactured in:
Sweden

Bodywork
Assembled/Manufactured in:
United Kingdom

The N113 is the successful replacement for the N112 chassis and comes in many different forms. Among the varieties are the single-deck step-entrance, double deckers and the low-floor single-deck models.

Scania provide one of their own 11 litre engines usually coupled to a Voith automatic gearbox.

The double deckers carried Alexander, East Lancs or Northern Counties bodies. Single deckers had East Lancs, Alexander, Wright or Plaxton bodywork while low-floor options included East Lancs, Alexander and Wrights. The vehicle shown is an N113CRB with an Alexander PS body.

Scania N270UD

Chassis
Assembled/Manufactured in:
Sweden

Bodywork
Assembled/Manufactured in:
United Kingdom

Description

Scania's N270 is available as either a double-deck (UD) or single-deck (UB) conventional two-axle chassis. The 270 designation in the chassis code denotes the engine horsepower rating.

This Scania chassis comes in varying lengths depending on its application. Double deckers are 10.7 m long, articulated vehicles are 18 m, while single deckers vary from 10.5 m to 12.8 m. The N270's ZF gearbox is driven by one of Scania's own diesel engines although alternative fuel options are available.

Alexander Dennis offer their Enviro400 bodywork on this chassis, while Optare offer the Olympus which was originally an East Lancashire Coachbuilders product. Another East Lancs design available is the OmniDekka which latterly became available as the Optare OmniDekka.

34

Scania OmniCity

Chassis
Assembled/Manufactured in:
Sweden

Bodywork
Assembled/Manufactured in:
Poland, Russia and Sweden

The OmniCity is an integral product originally built for the European market. It was later made available as a low-floor city bus in the United Kingdom.

The OmniCity is supplied with one of Scania's own engines attached to a ZF automatic gearbox. The standard single decker comes as a 12 m model while the articulated version is 18 m long and the double decker is 10.6 m.

The bodywork is now built by Omni Katrineholm AB, a wholly owned subsidiary of Scania. Although Omni now build buses in Poland and Russia, originally the OmniCity body was built in Sweden.

35

Volvo Ailsa

Chassis
Assembled/Manufactured in:
United Kingdom

Bodywork
Assembled/Manufactured in:
United Kingdom

Description

Although called a Volvo, the bus was conceived and built by the Ailsa Bus Company, eventually becoming part of Volvo itself.

The Ailsa unusually has a front-mounted Volvo turbocharged engine and a Self-Changing Gears gearbox. With the updated Mark II the option of a Voith gearbox also became available. The Mark III was originally planned to be called the Volvo B55; however, the Ailsa name continued to be used.

Ailsa models have either Northern Counties, Van Hool-McArdle, Marshall, East Lancs or Alexander bodywork, the most numerous by a large margin being Alexander. The vehicle shown is a unique Alexander variation for London Buses with two staircases and a door at both front and rear. It carried fleet number V3.

36

Volvo B6B

Chassis
Assembled/Manufactured in:
United Kingdom

Bodywork
Assembled/Manufactured in:
United Kingdom

Description

The Volvo B6B was designed as a competitor to Dennis's successful Dart. It would also eventually be available as a low-floor model – the B6LE.

B6s have one of Volvo's own engines coupled to either a ZF or Allison gearbox. It could also be found as a small coach with manual transmission.

Step-entrance models have bodywork built by Alexander, Marshall, Northern Counties and Plaxton. The low-floor version, the B6LE, was bodied by Plaxton, East Lancs and Wrights. The two B6Bs shown carry Plaxton Pointer bodywork, a design that was originally intended for the Dennis Dart.

37

Volvo B7RLE

Chassis
Assembled/Manufactured in:
Sweden

Bodywork
Assembled/Manufactured in:
Republic of Ireland

The B7RLE is a low-entrance version of the already successful B7R which was designed for long-distance and tourist work, although it has been used successfully as an inter-city bus.

The chassis design of the B7RLE allows low access to the front and centre doors with an advertised ground clearance of 320 mm above the road surface. Supplied as standard with one of Volvo's own engines, choices of ZF 6-speed or Voith 4-speed gearboxes are available.

The vehicle shown has a Wright Eclipse body which shares its styling with the Meridian on the MAN A22 chassis and the Solar on the Scania K230 chassis. Other bodywork options for the B7RLE include the Alexander Dennis Enviro300, Optare Esteem and Plaxton Centro.

38

Volvo B9TL

Chassis
Assembled/Manufactured in:
Sweden

Bodywork
Assembled/Manufactured in:
Republic of Ireland

Description

The Volvo B9TL is a low-floor chassis designed for double-deck bodywork. Despite being a city bus these vehicles do appear on longer-distance routes with some operators.

The B9TL is fitted with either the Volvo D9A or D9B engine, coupled to a ZF 6-speed or a Voith 4-speed automatic gearbox.

The vehicle shown has a Wright Eclipse Gemini body, which shares its styling with Wright's own Gemini 2 and the Pulsar Gemini. Alternative bodywork options for the B9TL are the Alexander Dennis Enviro400, Optare's Olympus and the open-top Visionaire.

39

Volvo B10BLE

Chassis
Assembled/Manufactured in:
Sweden

Bodywork
Assembled/Manufactured in:
Republic of Ireland

Description

The B10BLE is the low-entrance variation in Volvo's B10 range of chassis, replacing the step-entrance B10B and since superseded by the B7RLE.

The B10BLE has one of Volvo's own engines, mounted on the rear overhang; it is usually coupled to a ZF gearbox.

One of the more common choices of bodywork for the B10BLE in the United Kingdom is the Wright Renown, shown opposite. A similar body can be mounted on Volvo's B10L and Scania chassis. Other body options found on the B10BLE include Alexander's ALX300 design and the Plaxton Prestige.

40

Volvo Citybus

Chassis
Assembled/Manufactured in:
Scotland/Sweden

Bodywork
Assembled/Manufactured in:
United Kingdom

The Citybus was conceived by Ailsa and sold under the Volvo name. It was originally built in Scotland, but after a short time the decision was made to switch production to Sweden.

The design utilises a chassis based on the earlier Ailsa models with its running units taken from Volvo's standard B10M. Citybus chassis have an automatic gearbox driven by a 9.6 litre Volvo engine.

Strathclyde PTE took the prototype which had a body built by Marshall, which also built production vehicles for Derby. Other bodybuilders include Alexander, Northern Counties and East Lancashire, which built this Network Colchester example.

Volvo
Olympian

Chassis
Assembled/Manufactured in:
United Kingdom

Bodywork
Assembled/Manufactured in:
United Kingdom

Description

When Volvo acquired Leyland Bus in 1988 the right to produce the Olympian was part of the deal. Initially chassis were still produced under the Leyland name but after modifications it was re-launched as the Volvo Olympian.

The Volvo Olympian was originally available with a choice of a Cummins or Volvo engine, although on later models only the Volvo was offered. The standard gearbox was either Voith or ZF.

The vehicle shown has a Northern Counties Palatine II body. Options were the Alexander R-type and Royale along with East Lancs E-type and Pyoneer.

42

VDL SB200

Chassis
Assembled/Manufactured in:
Netherlands

Bodywork
Assembled/Manufactured in:
Republic of Ireland

VDL became a bus manufacturer when they took over DAF Bus International which included the chassis designs already in production. One of these was the DAF SB200 which was the replacement for the SB220.

These lightweight 11.9 m city buses are powered by Cummins engines driving a Voith gearbox. They were originally designed for Arriva, the VDL UK dealers.

The SB200 is available with Plaxton Centro bodywork or Wright Commander which was superseded by the Pulsar. The vehicle shown is a Pulsar 2 which can be differentiated from the earlier design by its new-style headlights similar to those fitted on Wright's Streetcar.

43

Wright Gemini 2

Chassis
Assembled/Manufactured in:
Netherlands

Bodywork
Assembled/Manufactured in:
Republic of Ireland

The Gemini 2 is a Wright product which has running units manufactured by Van der Leegte. These vehicles are available both as hybrids or with diesel engines.

On hybrid models power is supplied by a 2.4 litre Ford Puma engine to charge the traction batteries. Diesel vehicles have a 6.7 litre Cummins engine coupled to either a ZF or Voith gearbox, depending on the buyer's preference.

The rear of the hybrid is distinctive in having large grilles on the offside rear corner to aid cooling of the batteries. The front styling is very similar to Wright's other Gemini products.

Wright Streetcar

Chassis
Assembled/Manufactured in:
Sweden

Bodywork
Assembled/Manufactured in:
Republic of Ireland

Description

The Streetcar was designed to bridge the gap between the bus and the light rail system, with the claim that a complete system would be at a tenth of the cost. The 'ftr', which stands for 'future', was created as a joint venture between First Buses and Wright's bodybuilders. It also requires the co-operation of the local transport authority to reach its potential by creating dedicated rights of way.

The ftrs were originally built on a modified B7LA, although Volvo has now ceased production of that chassis, so all new vehicles will be on the B9LA variant with similar adaptations. The radiator has been moved from its position above the vertically mounted engine in the nearside rear corner and is now roof-mounted, allowing a full-width rear window.

The vehicle shown has the standard Wright streetcar body which only seats 37 passengers although it provides room for 76 standing.

Bus Talk

Some of the terms in this book are specific to the transport – or more especially to the bus – industry. The following may help to explain:

Chassis   The vehicle's rigid frame and mechanical components such as the engine, gearbox, suspension, differentials, drive shafts and axles.

Bodywork   The structure that is attached to the chassis to accommodate the driver and passengers.

Integral   A vehicle which has the chassis frame and components built into the bodywork structure.

Step-entrance   A vehicle which has one or more steps at the entrance door. Buses are no longer built in this form.

Low-floor   A bus with an entrance and some seats accessible without a step. These buses often have the ability to lower suspension to aid access.

Hybrid   A bus using some form of electric technology to provide power and reduce carbon emissions. Many variations currently exist.

Also in the 'Know Your' series...

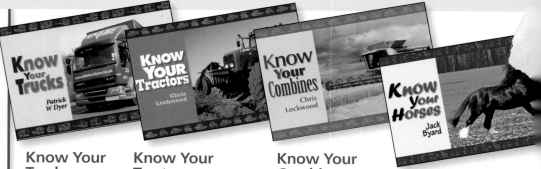

Know Your Trucks
Partrick W Dyer
Patrick Dyer has selected 44 examples to show the wide range of truck types you are likely to see on British roads

Know Your Tractors
Chris Lockwood
Chris Lockwood presents many of the most popular tractors that are in use around Britain today. Each of them features a detailed description and a full-page photograph.

Know Your Combines
Chris Lockwood
The author shows a representative sample of the combine harvesters which are most likely to be currently seen working in Britain's fields.

Know Your Horses
Jack Byard
This book provides a detailed description as well as a full-page photograph of each breed mentioned. The author describes the animal's appearance, its uses and history.

£4.99 e<